EMMANUEL JOSEPH

The Arc of Fulfillment, Integrating Financial Wisdom, Personal Wellness, and Relationship Harmony

Copyright © 2025 by Emmanuel Joseph

All rights reserved. No part of this publication may be reproduced, stored or transmitted in any form or by any means, electronic, mechanical, photocopying, recording, scanning, or otherwise without written permission from the publisher. It is illegal to copy this book, post it to a website, or distribute it by any other means without permission.

First edition

This book was professionally typeset on Reedsy. Find out more at reedsy.com

Contents

1	Chapter 1: The Foundations of Financial Wisdom	1
2	Chapter 2: Cultivating a Wealth Mindset	3
3	Chapter 3: Mastering Personal Wellness	5
4	Chapter 4: The Power of Relationship Harmony	7
5	Chapter 5: The Balance Between Work and Play	9
6	Chapter 6: Financial Planning for the Future	11
7	Chapter 7: The Importance of Self-Care	13
8	Chapter 8: Building Financial Resilience	15
9	Chapter 9: Nurturing Mental Health	17
10	Chapter 10: The Role of Gratitude in Fulfillment	19
11	Chapter 11: Effective Communication for Relationship Success	21
12	Chapter 12: The Synergy of Mind, Body, and Spirit	23
13	Chapter 13: The Power of Positive Thinking	25
14	Chapter 14: The Art of Letting Go	27
15	Chapter 15: The Journey to Fulfillment	29

1

Chapter 1: The Foundations of Financial Wisdom

The journey to financial wisdom begins with understanding the fundamental principles of money management. It's not just about accumulating wealth, but about making informed decisions that lead to long-term financial stability. This requires a comprehensive understanding of budgeting, saving, and investing. Setting clear financial goals is essential, as it provides a roadmap for where you want to be in the future. These goals should be realistic and achievable, taking into account your current financial situation and future aspirations.

A crucial aspect of financial wisdom is the ability to distinguish between needs and wants. This involves a conscious effort to prioritize essential expenses over discretionary ones. By doing so, you can ensure that your financial resources are allocated effectively, allowing you to build a solid financial foundation. Additionally, understanding the impact of compound interest and the importance of early saving can significantly enhance your financial trajectory. It's never too early to start planning for retirement, and small, consistent contributions can grow substantially over time.

Another important element is learning to manage debt wisely. Not all debt is bad, but it's crucial to differentiate between good debt, such as a mortgage or student loan, and bad debt, like high-interest credit card balances. Developing a strategy to pay off high-interest debt quickly can save you a significant amount of money in the long run. Furthermore, maintaining a good credit score is vital, as it affects your ability to borrow money at favorable terms in the future. Regularly monitoring your credit report and addressing any discrepancies can help you maintain a healthy credit profile.

Lastly, financial wisdom involves a continuous process of education and adaptation. The financial landscape is constantly evolving, and staying informed about changes in the economy, tax laws, and investment opportunities is crucial. Engaging with financial literature, attending workshops, and seeking advice from financial professionals can provide valuable insights and help you make informed decisions. By cultivating a mindset of lifelong learning, you can navigate the complexities of personal finance with confidence and achieve lasting financial stability.

2

Chapter 2: Cultivating a Wealth Mindset

Developing a wealth mindset is crucial to achieving financial success. It starts with understanding that wealth is not merely the accumulation of money but a state of mind that values abundance and opportunity. A positive outlook on financial matters can significantly impact your ability to attract and retain wealth. This mindset involves believing in your capability to achieve financial goals and recognizing that setbacks are merely stepping stones to greater achievements.

One essential aspect of a wealth mindset is the practice of gratitude. Regularly acknowledging and appreciating what you have, regardless of your current financial situation, can create a sense of abundance. This practice shifts your focus from scarcity and lack to opportunities and possibilities. By being grateful for small financial victories, you cultivate a mindset that attracts more wealth into your life. Additionally, visualizing your financial goals and creating a vision board can serve as a powerful motivator to stay focused on your path to financial success.

Another key component is the willingness to take calculated risks. Building wealth often requires stepping out of your comfort zone and exploring new opportunities. This could mean investing in stocks, starting a business, or pursuing a higher-paying job. However, it's important to balance risk-taking with careful planning and research. Understanding the potential rewards and drawbacks of each opportunity allows you to make informed decisions and minimize financial losses. A wealth mindset embraces the idea that growth often involves taking well-considered risks.

Finally, surrounding yourself with like-minded individuals who share your financial goals can greatly influence your wealth mindset. Networking with successful people, joining financial literacy groups, or finding a mentor can provide valuable insights and support. Engaging in discussions about financial strategies and learning from others' experiences can help you stay motivated and inspired. By building a supportive community, you create an environment that nurtures your financial aspirations and encourages continuous growth.

3

Chapter 3: Mastering Personal Wellness

Personal wellness is a multifaceted concept that encompasses physical, mental, and emotional health. Achieving a state of well-being requires a holistic approach that addresses all aspects of your life. Physical wellness involves maintaining a healthy lifestyle through regular exercise, a balanced diet, and adequate sleep. Engaging in activities that promote physical health not only improves your overall well-being but also boosts your energy levels and productivity.

Mental wellness is equally important and involves managing stress, fostering a positive mindset, and engaging in intellectually stimulating activities. Practicing mindfulness and meditation can help reduce stress and increase mental clarity. Additionally, setting aside time for hobbies, reading, and learning new skills can keep your mind active and engaged. It's essential to recognize the signs of mental fatigue and take proactive steps to address them, such as seeking professional help or talking to a trusted friend or family member.

Emotional wellness involves understanding and managing your emotions effectively. This requires self-awareness and the ability to process and express feelings in a healthy manner. Building strong emotional resilience can help you navigate life's challenges with a positive outlook. Developing healthy coping mechanisms, such as journaling, practicing gratitude, and engaging in creative outlets, can significantly enhance your emotional well-being.

Additionally, fostering meaningful relationships and maintaining a support system can provide emotional stability and comfort.

Incorporating wellness practices into your daily routine is essential for maintaining a balanced and fulfilling life. This might include setting aside time for self-care, such as taking a walk, practicing yoga, or enjoying a hobby. Prioritizing wellness not only enhances your quality of life but also empowers you to pursue your goals with greater focus and determination. By committing to a holistic approach to wellness, you can achieve a harmonious balance that supports your overall happiness and fulfillment.

4

Chapter 4: The Power of Relationship Harmony

Strong and harmonious relationships are a cornerstone of a fulfilling life. They provide emotional support, companionship, and a sense of belonging. Building and maintaining healthy relationships requires effective communication, empathy, and mutual respect. Open and honest communication is the foundation of any successful relationship. It involves actively listening to others, expressing your thoughts and feelings clearly, and resolving conflicts in a constructive manner.

Empathy plays a crucial role in fostering relationship harmony. Understanding and appreciating the perspectives and emotions of others can strengthen your connections and build trust. Practicing empathy involves being present and attentive during interactions, validating others' feelings, and showing genuine concern for their well-being. By cultivating empathy, you can create a supportive and nurturing environment where relationships can thrive.

Mutual respect is another key element in maintaining harmonious relationships. This involves valuing each other's opinions, boundaries, and individuality. Respectful relationships are built on a foundation of trust and equality, where both parties feel valued and heard. It's important to address any issues or misunderstandings promptly and respectfully, ensuring that both parties feel respected and understood. By fostering a culture of mutual respect, you can create lasting and meaningful connections.

Lastly, investing time and effort in nurturing your relationships is essential for maintaining harmony. This might involve spending quality time together, engaging in shared activities, or simply showing appreciation and gratitude for each other. Celebrating each other's successes and providing support during challenging times can strengthen your bond and create a sense of unity. By prioritizing your relationships and putting in the effort to nurture them, you can achieve a state of harmony that enhances your overall fulfillment and happiness.

5

Chapter 5: The Balance Between Work and Play

Striking a balance between work and play is essential for leading a fulfilling life. This balance ensures that you remain productive while also enjoying moments of relaxation and recreation. It begins with setting clear boundaries between work and personal time. Establishing a designated workspace and adhering to a schedule can help create a healthy separation. This approach prevents work from encroaching on personal time and vice versa, allowing you to be fully present in both aspects of your life.

Time management is a crucial skill for achieving this balance. Prioritizing tasks based on their importance and deadlines can help you focus on what truly matters. Utilizing tools like planners, calendars, and task management apps can streamline your workflow and reduce stress. It's important to allocate time for breaks and leisure activities, as they can enhance your overall productivity and well-being. Engaging in activities that bring joy and relaxation, such as hobbies, exercise, or spending time with loved ones, can rejuvenate your mind and body.

Another key aspect is learning to say no. Overcommitting to work or social obligations can lead to burnout and diminish the quality of your personal life. It's essential to recognize your limits and prioritize self-care. By being selective about the commitments you take on, you can ensure that you have enough time and energy for both work and play. Communicating your boundaries to colleagues, friends, and family members can also help manage expectations and create a supportive environment.

Finally, embracing flexibility is important for maintaining a healthy work-play balance. Life is unpredictable, and there will be times when work demands more attention or personal matters take precedence. Being adaptable and willing to adjust your schedule can help you navigate these fluctuations with ease. Regularly reassessing your priorities and making necessary adjustments can ensure that you maintain a harmonious balance that supports your overall well-being.

6

Chapter 6: Financial Planning for the Future

Effective financial planning is essential for achieving long-term financial stability and fulfilling your life goals. It begins with assessing your current financial situation, including your income, expenses, assets, and liabilities. Creating a comprehensive budget can help you track your spending and identify areas where you can cut costs. This process allows you to allocate resources towards savings, investments, and debt repayment, setting the stage for a secure financial future.

Setting specific financial goals is a critical component of financial planning. These goals should be realistic, measurable, and time-bound, encompassing short-term, medium-term, and long-term objectives. Short-term goals might include building an emergency fund or paying off credit card debt, while medium-term goals could involve saving for a down payment on a house or funding a child's education. Long-term goals often focus on retirement planning and ensuring financial independence in your later years.

Diversifying your investments is another key element of financial planning. A well-balanced investment portfolio can help mitigate risks and maximize returns. This might include a mix of stocks, bonds, mutual funds, and real estate. Regularly reviewing and adjusting your investment strategy based on market conditions and your changing financial goals is crucial for maintaining a healthy portfolio. Seeking advice from financial professionals can provide valuable insights and help you make informed investment decisions.

Lastly, staying informed about changes in the financial landscape is essential for effective financial planning. This includes staying updated on tax laws, interest rates, and economic trends that may impact your financial situation. Engaging in continuous financial education through books, seminars, and online resources can enhance your financial literacy and empower you to make better decisions. By adopting a proactive approach to financial planning, you can achieve your financial goals and enjoy a secure and prosperous future.

7

Chapter 7: The Importance of Self-Care

Self-care is a vital aspect of maintaining overall well-being and achieving a balanced life. It involves taking deliberate actions to nurture your physical, mental, and emotional health. Prioritizing self-care can help reduce stress, increase resilience, and improve your overall quality of life. It starts with recognizing the importance of self-care and making a commitment to incorporate it into your daily routine.

Physical self-care involves activities that promote bodily health, such as regular exercise, a balanced diet, and adequate sleep. Engaging in physical activities that you enjoy, whether it's yoga, running, or dancing, can boost your energy levels and improve your mood. Additionally, nourishing your body with healthy, nutrient-rich foods can enhance your overall well-being. Ensuring you get enough rest and sleep is also crucial for maintaining physical health and rejuvenating your mind and body.

Mental self-care focuses on activities that stimulate your mind and promote mental clarity. This might include reading, solving puzzles, or engaging in creative pursuits. Practicing mindfulness and meditation can help calm your mind and reduce stress. It's important to set aside time for activities that challenge your intellect and encourage personal growth. Taking regular breaks from work and digital devices can also help prevent mental fatigue and promote mental wellness.

Emotional self-care involves understanding and managing your emotions effectively. This includes expressing your feelings, seeking support from loved ones, and engaging in activities that bring you joy. Building strong emotional resilience can help you navigate life's challenges with a positive outlook. Developing healthy coping mechanisms, such as journaling, practicing gratitude, and engaging in creative outlets, can significantly enhance your emotional well-being. By prioritizing self-care, you can achieve a harmonious balance that supports your overall happiness and fulfillment.

8

Chapter 8: Building Financial Resilience

Financial resilience is the ability to withstand and recover from financial setbacks. It involves developing strategies to protect yourself from unexpected financial challenges and ensuring that you can maintain stability during difficult times. One key aspect of financial resilience is building an emergency fund. This fund should cover at least three to six months' worth of living expenses, providing a safety net in case of job loss, medical emergencies, or other unforeseen circumstances.

Another important element is diversifying your income sources. Relying on a single source of income can be risky, especially in uncertain economic times. Exploring additional income streams, such as freelance work, part-time jobs, or passive income opportunities, can enhance your financial stability. Having multiple income sources can help you weather financial storms and reduce the impact of any single income disruption.

Insurance is also a critical component of financial resilience. Health, life, disability, and property insurance can protect you and your family from significant financial losses. Regularly reviewing and updating your insurance policies ensures that you have adequate coverage for your needs. Additionally, understanding the terms and conditions of your policies can help you make informed decisions and avoid unexpected expenses.

Lastly, cultivating a mindset of financial resilience involves staying informed and adaptable. Keeping up-to-date with economic trends, financial news, and changes in the job market can help you anticipate potential challenges and take proactive measures. Developing a flexible financial plan that can be adjusted as circumstances change is essential for maintaining long-term stability. By building financial resilience, you can confidently navigate life's uncertainties and achieve lasting financial well-being.

9

Chapter 9: Nurturing Mental Health

Mental health is a crucial aspect of overall well-being, influencing how we think, feel, and act. It affects our ability to cope with stress, relate to others, and make decisions. Nurturing mental health requires a proactive approach, including self-awareness, self-care, and seeking support when needed. Recognizing the signs of mental health challenges, such as anxiety, depression, or burnout, is the first step in addressing them.

Practicing mindfulness and meditation can significantly improve mental health. These practices involve focusing on the present moment and cultivating a sense of calm and clarity. Mindfulness techniques, such as deep breathing exercises, can help reduce stress and promote relaxation. Additionally, engaging in activities that bring joy and fulfillment, such as hobbies, socializing, or spending time in nature, can enhance mental well-being.

Building a strong support network is also essential for nurturing mental health. Surrounding yourself with supportive friends, family members, and colleagues can provide emotional comfort and encouragement. Openly discussing your feelings and challenges with trusted individuals can help alleviate stress and foster a sense of connection. Seeking professional help, such as therapy or counseling, can provide valuable insights and coping strategies for managing mental health issues.

Lastly, maintaining a healthy lifestyle can have a positive impact on mental health. Regular physical activity, a balanced diet, and adequate sleep contribute to overall well-being and resilience. Avoiding harmful habits, such as excessive alcohol consumption or drug use, is crucial for maintaining mental health. By prioritizing mental health and adopting a holistic approach, you can achieve a balanced and fulfilling life.

10

Chapter 10: The Role of Gratitude in Fulfillment

Gratitude is a powerful emotion that can significantly enhance your overall sense of fulfillment. It involves recognizing and appreciating the positive aspects of your life, no matter how small they may seem. Practicing gratitude can shift your focus from what you lack to what you have, fostering a sense of abundance and contentment. This positive outlook can improve your mental and emotional well-being and strengthen your relationships.

One effective way to practice gratitude is by keeping a gratitude journal. Writing down three things you are grateful for each day can help you develop a habit of focusing on the positive. Reflecting on these moments can increase your overall happiness and resilience. Additionally, expressing gratitude to others, whether through verbal acknowledgment or written notes, can deepen your connections and create a sense of mutual appreciation.

Gratitude can also enhance your financial well-being. By appreciating what you have and being content with your current financial situation, you can reduce the urge to engage in unnecessary spending. This mindful approach to finances can help you make more intentional and informed decisions, leading to greater financial stability. Practicing gratitude can also motivate you to give back to others, whether through charitable donations or acts of kindness, creating a positive impact on your community.

Incorporating gratitude into your daily life requires a conscious effort to focus on the positive aspects of each day. This practice can be as simple as taking a few moments each morning or evening to reflect on what you are thankful for. Over time, gratitude can become a natural part of your mindset, enhancing your overall sense of fulfillment and happiness. By embracing gratitude, you can create a life filled with joy, appreciation, and meaningful connections.

11

Chapter 11: Effective Communication for Relationship Success

Effective communication is the cornerstone of successful relationships. It involves not only expressing your thoughts and feelings clearly but also listening actively to others. Open and honest communication fosters trust, understanding, and connection. Developing strong communication skills requires practice and a conscious effort to improve.

Active listening is a crucial component of effective communication. It involves paying full attention to the speaker, making eye contact, and providing verbal and non-verbal feedback. This demonstrates that you value and respect their perspective. Reflective listening, where you paraphrase or summarize what the speaker has said, can help clarify understanding and show that you are engaged in the conversation. By practicing active listening, you can build stronger, more meaningful connections.

Another key aspect is expressing yourself clearly and assertively. This involves being honest about your thoughts and feelings while respecting the other person's viewpoint. Using "I" statements, such as "I feel" or "I think," can help convey your message without sounding accusatory or confrontational. It's also important to be mindful of your tone and body language, as they can significantly impact how your message is received. Clear and assertive communication can help resolve conflicts and strengthen relationships.

Empathy and compassion play a vital role in effective communication. Understanding and acknowledging the emotions of others can foster a sense of connection and trust. Practicing empathy involves being present, showing genuine interest, and validating the other person's feelings. Compassionate communication also involves offering support and encouragement when needed. By cultivating empathy and compassion, you can create a safe and nurturing environment where relationships can thrive.

12

Chapter 12: The Synergy of Mind, Body, and Spirit

Achieving overall well-being requires a harmonious balance between mind, body, and spirit. This holistic approach recognizes that these three aspects are interconnected and influence each other. Nurturing each aspect can enhance your overall health and fulfillment. The synergy of mind, body, and spirit involves practices that promote mental clarity, physical vitality, and spiritual growth.

Mental well-being is fostered through practices that stimulate and relax the mind. Engaging in intellectually stimulating activities, such as reading, learning new skills, and solving puzzles, can keep your mind sharp. Mindfulness and meditation can promote mental clarity and reduce stress. Regularly setting aside time for self-reflection and journaling can also enhance your mental well-being. By prioritizing mental health, you can achieve a balanced and focused mindset.

Physical well-being involves maintaining a healthy lifestyle through regular exercise, a balanced diet, and adequate sleep. Physical activity not only improves bodily health but also boosts mental and emotional well-being. Nourishing your body with nutrient-rich foods can enhance your energy levels and overall vitality. Ensuring you get enough rest and sleep is essential for rejuvenating your mind and body. By prioritizing physical health, you can achieve a state of vitality and resilience.

Spiritual well-being involves practices that nurture your inner self and provide a sense of purpose and connection. This might include engaging in spiritual or religious practices, spending time in nature, or pursuing activities that bring you joy and fulfillment. Connecting with your inner self through meditation, prayer, or contemplation can foster a sense of peace and alignment. Building a strong sense of community and engaging in acts of kindness can also enhance your spiritual well-being. By nurturing your spirit, you can achieve a sense of purpose and fulfillment.

13

Chapter 13: The Power of Positive Thinking

Positive thinking is a powerful tool that can significantly impact your overall well-being and success. It involves cultivating an optimistic mindset and focusing on the positive aspects of life. This mindset can improve your mental and emotional health, enhance your relationships, and increase your resilience. Developing a habit of positive thinking requires practice and a conscious effort to shift your perspective.

One effective way to cultivate positive thinking is through affirmations. Positive affirmations are statements that reinforce your strengths, capabilities, and goals. Repeating affirmations daily can help reprogram your mind to focus on the positive and build self-confidence. Visualizing your goals and success can also enhance your motivation and determination. By regularly practicing affirmations and visualization, you can create a positive mindset that supports your aspirations.

Another key aspect is reframing negative thoughts. It's natural to experience negative thoughts and emotions, but learning to reframe them can help you maintain a positive outlook. This involves challenging negative beliefs and replacing them with more constructive and empowering ones. For example, instead of thinking "I can't do this," reframe it as "I can learn and improve." Practicing gratitude can also help shift your focus from what you lack to what you have, fostering a sense of abundance and contentment.

Surrounding yourself with positive influences is crucial for maintaining a positive mindset. This includes spending time with supportive and uplifting people, engaging in activities that bring you joy, and consuming positive and inspiring content. Creating a positive environment can reinforce your optimistic outlook and motivate you to pursue your goals. By embracing positive thinking, you can enhance your overall well-being and achieve greater success and fulfillment.

14

Chapter 14: The Art of Letting Go

Letting go is an essential skill for achieving emotional freedom and personal growth. It involves releasing attachments to past experiences, negative emotions, and limiting beliefs. The art of letting go requires self-awareness, acceptance, and a willingness to move forward. By letting go of what no longer serves you, you can create space for new opportunities and experiences.

Self-awareness is the first step in the process of letting go. This involves recognizing the thoughts, emotions, and behaviors that hold you back. Reflecting on past experiences and identifying patterns can help you understand the root causes of your attachments. Journaling, meditation, and self-reflection are effective tools for increasing self-awareness. By gaining clarity about what you need to let go of, you can take proactive steps towards emotional freedom.

Acceptance is a crucial component of letting go. It involves acknowledging and embracing your emotions without judgment. This means allowing yourself to feel and process your emotions fully, rather than suppressing or denying them. Acceptance also involves recognizing that the past cannot be changed and that holding onto negative emotions can hinder your growth. By accepting your experiences and emotions, you can release their hold on you and move forward.

The willingness to move forward is the final step in the process of letting go. This requires a conscious decision to release attachments and embrace new possibilities. Practicing forgiveness, both for yourself and others, can help you let go of resentment and anger. Cultivating a mindset of gratitude and focusing on the present moment can also support your journey towards emotional freedom. By mastering the art of letting go, you can achieve a state of inner peace and personal growth.

15

Chapter 15: The Journey to Fulfillment

The journey to fulfillment is a continuous process of growth, self-discovery, and alignment with your true self. It involves integrating financial wisdom, personal wellness, and relationship harmony to create a balanced and fulfilling life. This journey requires a commitment to self-improvement, a willingness to embrace change, and an openness to new experiences.

Setting meaningful goals is an essential part of the journey to fulfillment. These goals should reflect your values, passions, and aspirations. Taking the time to reflect on what truly matters to you can help you identify and prioritize your goals. Creating a vision board or writing a personal mission statement can serve as a powerful reminder of your purpose and direction. By aligning your goals with your true self, you can create a life that brings you joy and satisfaction.

Embracing change is another key aspect of the journey to fulfillment. Life is dynamic, and change is inevitable. Developing a mindset of adaptability and resilience can help you navigate life's challenges and seize new opportunities. This involves being open to new experiences, learning from setbacks, and continuously evolving. By embracing change, you can create a life that is rich with growth and possibilities.

The book description

In "The Arc of Fulfillment," embark on a transformative journey towards a balanced and enriching life. This insightful guide weaves together the essential elements of financial wisdom, personal wellness, and relationship harmony, offering practical advice and profound insights to help you achieve lasting fulfillment.

Discover the foundational principles of money management and learn how to build a secure financial future through budgeting, saving, and investing wisely. Cultivate a wealth mindset that embraces abundance and opportunity, and master the art of financial planning to ensure stability and growth.

Nurture your physical, mental, and emotional well-being with holistic approaches to personal wellness. From maintaining a healthy lifestyle to practicing mindfulness and self-care, this book provides tools to enhance your overall quality of life and resilience.

Strengthen your connections with others by fostering relationship harmony. Explore the power of effective communication, empathy, and mutual respect in building strong and meaningful relationships. Learn how to balance work and play, prioritize self-care, and cultivate gratitude to create a life filled with joy, contentment, and meaningful connections.

"The Arc of Fulfillment" is your comprehensive guide to integrating financial wisdom, personal wellness, and relationship harmony, empowering you to lead a life of purpose, balance, and fulfillment. Unlock the secrets to a harmonious and prosperous life and embrace the journey towards your true potential.

www.ingramcontent.com/pod-product-compliance
Lightning Source LLC
LaVergne TN
LVHW020502080526
838202LV00057B/6116